Dunbar and District
in old picture postcards

by David M. Anderson

European Library ZALTBOMMEL/THE NETHERLANDS

Acknowledgements:
I would like to thank John T.
Harkess for pictures 26 and 30;
Thomas K. Anderson for pictures
25, 28, 39 and 43; the staff of the
Local History Centre, East Lothian
District Library Service; Dunbar
and District History Society; and all
those who have contributed
comments and suggestions.

For Lynsey, Kirsty and Islay.

GB ISBN 90 288 6232 3 / CIP

© 1996 European Library – Zaltbommel/The Netherlands

Introduction

In the early years of the 20th century Dunbar was a bustling, thriving place – at least in the summer tourist months. It gained this trade from its position on the east coast, thirty miles away from Edinburgh, and sold itself on its record-breaking hours of sunshine and breezy sea air. It was able to offer all sorts of outdoor amusements and with a number of sites of historic and natural interest nearby there was something for everyone. There was also a corresponding steady decline in the traditional industries of fishing and small scale manufacturing. Furthermore, increasing agricultural mechanisation was leading to steady reductions in the number of hands needed to work rich farmlands in surrounding districts. Great attempts were made to counter both trends by marketing and improving the available tourist attractions to secure employment, both in construction and in service industries. The whole character of the town and district was to become part of a tourist's experience – from the bustle of the harbours and the network of fields, steadings and villages to the people themselves. City folk were already separated from the sea and land, but remained fascinated by those who still toiled in traditional tasks.

It was usual for visitors to arrive by train. New arrivals to Dunbar's fine station would often be able to hear and scent part of that which would make many of them return and return. Because, surrounded as Dunbar is by a broken and often rocky coast, the sound of the sea is seldom absent. Above all are cries of seabirds: cacophonous, squabbling, herring gulls in the town and the daintier, but equally noisy, onomatopoeic kittiwakes at their unique nesting ground on the face of the castle rock down by the shore. The steady summer breeze from the sea brings the taste of salt and after a storm the smell of tangle, cast-up seaweed, can be a bit of a shock to unsuspecting city dwellers! On departing the station visitors leave behind them the sweep of the Lammermuirs. The old, weathered range encloses and cradles the fertile Dunbar plain between its arms and promises productive, scenic trips to come. Glimpses of the town would be seen from the carriage or cab windows on the way to a hotel or rented home. Impressions might be gained of fine new villas, but also of older huddles of red sandstone buildings, a wide High Street and narrow wynds or vennels in the older part of the town.

A typical visitor might spend their first evening strolling or learning about local history from the Burgh Register or one of the many illustrated tourist guides. They might learn from their text of the powerful Earls of Dunbar, who challenged for the throne of Scotland, and one of their famous Countesses, 'Black Agnes' Randolph, who held the ancient castle against an English host. It was the castle around which the early history of Dunbar centred, but the Earls held great areas of land nearby. There were several smaller castles and tower houses within a few miles, protecting the fertile coastal plain. In the days of their strength, some of these were in the hands of trusted captains and others held by families related to the Earls to create a defence in depth in times of trouble. Similarly, several local chapels were brought into a subsidiary relationship to the Collegiate Church of Dunbar and in other places land was granted to monastic orders. The now peaceful land of East Lothian was fought over many times, in part owing to its strategic location near the border with England, but also due to its natural wealth. One nearby battlefield, where Cromwell scattered General Leslie's Scots army, was easily visited on a short walk from the town. The vantage point of Doon Hill, which the Scots had held, yields a panoramic view of the entire field (still remarkably free of modern development). The same vantage point serves to emphasise Dunbar's relationship with the sea and the variegated landscape of the coastal plain.

Guidebooks were particularly lyrical on the beauties of the surrounding countryside, some of the most productive and wealthy in Britain. Planning one's itinerary might take several pleasant hours. There were woodlands, valleys and beaches to visit. Many of the great country and mansion houses nearby had pleasure grounds and gardens in which visitors were encouraged at times to stroll. The villages surrounding Dunbar had a picturesque reputation all of their own. Of course, one might simply purchase one of the organised excursions that daily ran from the High Street or the main hotels to a variety of places in the county. In 1913 the St. George was able to offer four-in-hand pleasure excursions departing daily and carriages and motors for hire with experienced (and reliable) drivers.

'Dunbar in old picture postcards' presented the town in three walks as a visitor might experience it. This volume is laid out similarly and comprises three excursions interspersed with explorations within the burgh bounds of Dunbar. The first excursion starts out with a boat trip to the Bass Rock and Tantallon Castle, returning through an ancient pilgrimage site at Whitekirk, following the Tyne to East Linton and so to home by way of Belhaven. The second excursion heads south-east along the coast to Barns Ness, Skateraw, Cove, Pease Bay then back by way of Cockburnspath, Dunglass, Oldhamstocks and Innerwick. The third skirts the hills by passing through Spott, Stenton and Whittinge-hame, returning through the policies of Biel Estate. The scenes within Dunbar reprise parts of the first volume (well, it is only a wee place) but by using different pictures and many more can now be seen in the collection of the newly-formed Dunbar and District History Society. Then and now the High Street was familiar to everyone, with shops, restaurants and hotels. The Shore area was a source of novelty to young and old, who could explore at will the odd little passageways, or closes, and peer into the yards of several small businesses. Right by the coast were the hoary old castle ruins and Dunbar's chain of little interlinked harbours, where there was always something to see. The amusements laid on by the Town Council were popular ways to pass some time (especially for the many day-excursionists) and several cards have been selected to show the pools, putting greens and strolling places near the town. Changing fashions have meant that many of these last have disappeared in recent times. The magnificent Safety Swimming Pond has been completely removed and replaced with an indoor pool in an award winning 'modern' building. Golf has increased in popularity at the expense of the putting greens. Strolling places, such as the coastal promenades, have been allowed to degrade. In the years since these postcards were produced the town has expanded in area, sweeping in much once green land, forcing walkers much farther afield. Even the John Muir Country Park, named in honour of a Dunbar-born environmental activist, has a car park, although it is well used and the park suits the needs of present-day excursionists.

It is hoped that the pictures give an impression of a tourist's complete experience of Dunbar District in our grandfathers' day and not just grand ruins and fine houses. One or two of the photographs are rather plain. Their inclusion is justified for several reasons. There must have been a market for them when they were produced, however small, and it's difficult for a photographer to make dramatic shots of villages that were sleepy and quiet even a century ago. In many cases a card is from a short print run, made locally for distribution amongst a family or in anticipation of a large group of day-trippers, who might want a cheap remembrance. Whereas Dunbar had a full range of souvenirs, the little village stores might only run to some representative postcards. However, the range of small places for which cards are available is noteworthy. And it's lucky for us that the adventurous souls exploring the district in their carriages and charabancs were caught up in the great postcard collecting craze, for otherwise we might have no pictorial record at all!

1 It took only a few pence to hire a cabman or coachman at the railway station for a run up to the town. The entrance to the High Street might be quiet and still in the early morning; eerily empty. Perhaps there might be a haar, or sea-mist. A blanket of moist air often rolls in off the sea to muffle sound and writhe around the streetside lamps. When the sun rises the haar will burn off and the street takes on colour and depth. This photograph was taken in 1904. The single-storeyed General Post Office, part hidden by shuttering down the narrow street in the centre of the picture, was under construction. The new office was also a sorting office and telephone exchange and was needed to replace more cramped premises much further down the street.

2   As the day wears on, carters collect goods for delivery. Blinds sprout to protect window displays from the bright sun. The Town House is in the centre of the picture. Its tower carries two sundials and a clock. The administration of the burgh was centred here with court, council chamber, prison, police office and all the burgh officials. Dunbar seems to have had some sort of toll-booth or town house from the early sixteenth century. The building in the picture may date from the 1590s, but most authorities date it to the first decade of the seventeenth century. It is still in use and a part holds a very successful little museum. The provost, or mayor, when this photo was taken was George Low. His business premises are between the portico of the George Hotel and the chemist's shop (marked by the symbolic mortar and pestle).

HIGH ST. & TOWN HALL, DUNBAR.

3   The High Street gained its fine width from usage as a market place, before the mainly Victorian shop frontages were installed. Ages ago, the first fish landed at the havens was each day reserved by ordinance to be sold 'from the cross', i.e., at a prominent place in the street. Twice a year the hiring fair brought the countryside people to town to negotiate their next six months situation and the street became a fairground. This photographer captured the view on Victoria's diamond jubilee day, 22nd June 1897. Everyone was gathered to hear loyal proclamations and to promenade with friends. In the evening illuminated windows complemented the bunting and flags that decorated the frontages along the entire length. Note the seating provided as a special concession for the town's many veterans of Imperial service.

4   Visitors arriving at Dunbar for the season needed accommodation. Although a programme of hotel building led to lots of available rooms of all qualities, many preferred to rent a villa for a month or more. Just before the beginning of the 20th century there was a spate of building outside the old town boundaries, driven by demand in the summer months. A favourite location was East Links Road, where there were the Georgian Cottages, left, and one of these later Victorian terraced groups on the right. One of their selling points was direct access to the beach by means of gates and steps in the sea-wall behind. In the summer residents might retreat to a few rooms or an underflat to make room for the visitors, who often came with their entire household and servants. Miss Downie, a newsagent on the High Street, compiled a monthly register so that everybody knew who was staying where for their round of visiting (and social climbing).

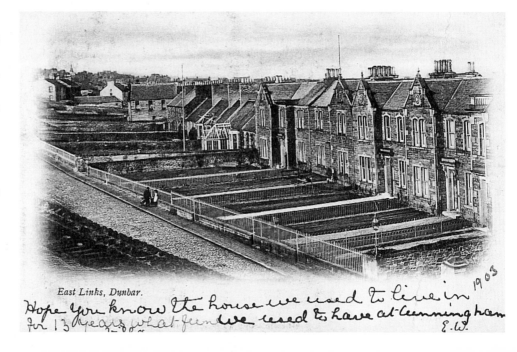

East Links, Dunbar.

Hope you know the house we used to live in 1903
for 13 years what fun we used to have at Cunningham
E.W.

5 This is one of the town's surviving hotels, although at present it hides under a different name. Dunbar was undergoing a boom in hotel building as the 20th century began. The Roxburghe, Bellevue, Kerridge's and the Royal (on the left of picture 1) were all open for business and doing very well catering to a wide range of customers. A number of other hotels such as the Albert or the Hillside subscribed to known standards for a particular clientele. Just as one knows what to expect at a 'Club Med' or 'Centre Parcs' of the present day, so it was then with a temperance hotel or a YMCA. Some of the hotels, the Roxburghe and Wilson's Temperance in particular, offered the whole health treatment. They had sea water baths, Russian baths, medicated baths, seaweed treatments, and a masseur and fitness expert. Not so very different from some places today. The Albert became, of course, the Goldenstones.

THE ALBERT HOTEL, DUNBAR.

A.4851.

6   The High Street was a hub where all the news (and gossip) could be relayed. These three gentlemen are standing outside No. 130-134, the childhood home of one of Dunbar's most famous sons. In 1838 John Muir was born next door at No. 128, but the family moved houses before he went to school. They moved again in 1849, all the way to Wisconsin, USA. In adulthood, John made his way to California, mostly by foot or by boat. He generated a reputation as a scientist and philosopher of the natural world, working in the High Sierra in all seasons. He is remembered today as the 'father of the conservation movement' for his work in the battles to create the American National Parks, the forerunner of all such institutions worldwide. His career was followed with great interest by contemporaries and old school friends in his native town, who were kept informed by relatives and copies of his publications. Perhaps John was being discussed here.

7   A walk about the town would be a good way for a visitor to get their bearings and the Castle Park might draw one's attention. It could not fail to if the militia was at big gun practice! In 1859 Lauderdale, or Dunbar, House was purchased by the War Department and became a barracks. A cadre of regular army gunners and service corpsmen was stationed in Dunbar to maintain a battery of 32 pounder guns, which were set on the headland beside the castle. Every summer Artillery Volunteer Regiments paraded to the town for their obligatory live firing at targets set out to sea. And every summer the fishers protested to anyone who would listen that the concussion of shot falling in the bay was driving away the fish (catches were declining). The Town Council was able to purchase some of these guns once they were obsolete, to stand as a remembrance on another clifftop site to the west.

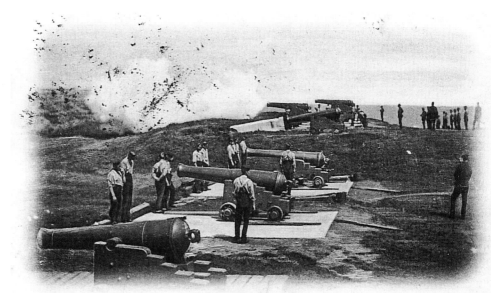

Big Gun Practice, Dunbar.

8 Amongst the castle's many tales and connections, that with the unhappy Mary Queen of Scots was often recalled. It was from here that she and Bothwell left on their journey that led to Carberry Hill and so to captivity for her and exile for him. That was in June 1567 and during 1568 the castle was finally slighted. Its defences were torn down by order of the Scottish Parliament to prevent it ever again standing against the authority of central government. From then on, one of Scotland's strongest fortresses was no more than a scenic ruin. It was about this time that probably the first breach was made in the curtain wall, shown above. If so, it is all the more remarkable that the wall held on until 1993 when it finally collapsed. At one time the wall protected the seaward part of the castle and contained a passageway communicating with a great bastion, which made the castle a fearsome prospect for an enemy to tackle.

Ruins of Watergate, where Queen Mary Escaped from Dunbar Castle

9   In this picture the bastion mentioned in the previous note towers over the Fisheries Board marine fish hatchery, accommodated in the sheds on the left. The bastion was a very early artillery emplacement and is still pierced with a tier of gunports, commanding all the landward approaches; at one time it is thought a further tier was above. The main part of the castle extended over what is now the harbour entrance, which was blasted through the living rock. The remains only hint at the strength of the fortress, but the sole inhabitants are nesting kittiwakes. These normally timid, retiring birds make this end of the harbour their own, bringing up their young on precarious ledges. There are many boats in this picture but the harbour still looks empty. It was busy only during the herring season and saw few merchant ships. Only a few in the potato and animal feed-stock trade could be called regular visitors and even those only in the appropriate season.

M. Wane & Co., Edinbro', No. 91.

Victoria Harbour,   Feb 13th 1904. every, every.   Dunbar.

10   The Bass Rock marks the mouth of the Firth of Forth. As an attraction, it is generally considered to fall into the sphere of Dunbar's great rival burgh North Berwick, the 'Biarritz of the North'. None the less, as can be seen from the inscription, a bit of poaching went on and it could be claimed by both places; the tradition is continued here. The rock, a vast volcanic neck over 300 feet high, presents the aspect of a vast water beetle, an impression only enhanced at dusk when the lighthouse gleams exactly where one might expect an eye. It is really too far from Dunbar for regular boat trips, as conditions can change extremely quickly.

However, fishermen would often chance out with a boat-load of sightseers. This happy set is just approaching the isle and will shortly appreciate its main attraction.

COPYRIGHT   THE BASS ROCK, DUNBAR. 59   SANSON'S SERIES DUNBAR

11   In September 1927 our boatload of excursionists might have diverted inshore to have a good look at the remains of the luckless S.S. Elterwater, ashore on the Carr Rocks under Seacliff. This card was sent not long after the wreck occurred, having been rushed out to record the event (it found its way to Dublin and someone who had helped launch the lifeboat) and before the vessel broke up and sank. A lot of local interest stemmed from the performance the salvage company went to in getting at the cargo, 3,000 tons of pig-iron. First they tried diving and then they tried a Witton-Kramer lifting magnet, manufactured by General Electric, mounted on the salvage vessel. Needless to say, this caused no end of comment, sucking of hollow teeth and knowing looks from the seawise fraternity; just like the concrete boat of many years later.

12   The vast white cliffs of the earlier picture resolve into a teeming mass of nesting seabirds. The Bass holds one of the foremost colonies of gannets, or Solan Geese. These birds are still familiar on in-shore waters as they plummet and dive for their food. This is their home and a trip to the Rock formed a highlight for the many naturalist and bird watching visitors to East Lothian (at another time a trip to the Bass meant food: eggs and seabirds salted or preserved in oil). Birds have sole dominion now the light has been automated, but once the Bass held a fortress, often used as a prison. A group of prisoners turned on their guards in 1691 and held the island for the exiled Stuarts until April 1694 – the last place in Britain to so hold out. The oldest references to the Bass concern the locally revered Saint Baldred, who is said to have died there; remarkably, three parishes claim his grave: a miracle meant each had a body to bury.

Sea Birds on Bass Rock

13　Phillimore of North Berwick published a unique series of postcards based on his own drawings. Their popularity stemmed from vignettes and tales tucked into odd corners, so the cards both entertained and informed. An entire book in this series is devoted to his cards. This example presents the formidable curtain wall of Tantallon Castle, another of the fine local fortresses. Behind the wall was a secure clifftop compound with a landing stage below. It was probably a Douglas family stronghold from its inception around 1370 and later it featured in the animosity between that family and James V, who eventually obtained it for himself. He needed to bribe the Governor of the castle to do so: 'ding doon Tantallon, build a brig to the Bass' is a local couplet celebrating two impossibilities, the first part meaning to take the castle by siege.

24(a) TANTALLON CASTLE

MARMION'S ESCAPE FROM TANTALLON

MARMION'S DEFIANCE

R·P·Phillimore

DOUGLAS　　MARMION

"The ponderous grate behind him rung"

"And when Lord Marmion reached his band
He halts & turns with clenched hands
And shout of loud defiance pours
And shook his gauntlet at the Towers."

Copyright Registered

14   Rural Whitekirk was originally the three parishes of Auldhame, Hamer and Tyninghame. The church and village of the first are lost. The hamlet of Tyninghame will be shown below. Hamer became Whitekirk and here is the ancient church of St. Mary. An early tradition of miracles mediated by a holy well encouraged a flow of pilgrims to the parish. The first is reputed to have been a Countess of Dunbar whose hurts were cured by drinking its water. Another became Pope Pius II (unfortunately, he came away with rheumatism) and large numbers of ordinary folk followed over the years. The visitors in 1914 were a little bit different because the church was set afire at night by suffragettes and the fire took a good grip before local people were roused to tackle it. Charles Bruce's photograph shows the smouldering aftermath. Many of the interior fittings were lost, but a sympathetic restoration by Robert Lorimer removed most traces of the damage.

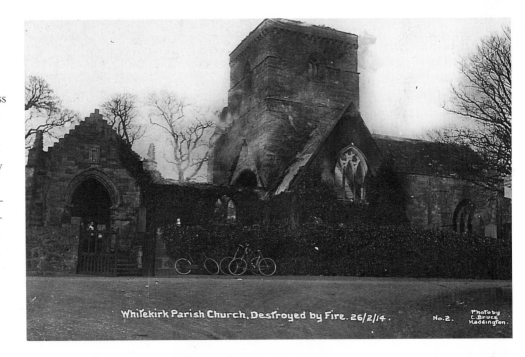

Whitekirk Parish Church, Destroyed by Fire. 26/2/14.   No.2.   Photo by C.Bruce Haddington.

15   Binning Woods lie between Tyninghame and Whitekirk. The woods and the park of Tyninghame House are the result of a pioneering planting commenced in the early 18th century by Thomas, Sixth Earl of Haddington. He was encouraged by his wife to embark on the project as an example of agricultural improvement and the result was hundreds of acres of broad leafed and evergreen forest interspersed with wide avenues and viewing points on a continental pattern. This early example was followed all over the county, which had been denuded of trees by extensive agricultural demands, to produce the variegated landscape of the present day. In Victorian times the estates were very popular sylvan resorts, where often trippers and picnickers from the cities were allowed to explore. Today they are reservoirs of wildlife and refuges for scarce red squirrels.

Binning Woods, near Dunbar.

16 The Earl of Haddington's great forestry project meant that the old village round the kirk of St. Baldred had to make way. Only parts of the kirk, reserved as the Earls' family burying place, remain to mark its site. A new village was built which today stands as the very model of an early nineteenth century rural development. Although built by different hands and at different times the buildings form a much admired and very popular whole. They run from a Factor's House and a Sawmill (for the estate) through terraces of cottages to a school and schoolhouse. One group is called Widows' Row, once occupied by retired estate labourers. Virtually all the inhabitants worked on the estate when this photo was taken; today most of them find employment away from the land or in the city.

Tyninghame Village

C. Hally & Son, East Linton

17   Preston Kirk gives its name to the surrounding parish although it has been called both Pestonhaugh and Lyntoun at different times. The kirk was originally dedicated to St. Baldred and old stories claim a statue of the saint stood in the kirkyard: its disappearance is put down to the stone being recycled for walling. Visitors came to see a fine old chancel dating from the 13th century, although like many of the local kirks this building was remodelled several times; in this case in both the 18th and 19th centuries. The kirkyard contains some fine old stones, amongst them that of Andrew Meikle. His claim to fame was as an agricultural engineer and mill-wright and it is fair to say that the equipment he developed gave Scottish farmers a technological edge. It is said there were over 600 threshing mills of his pattern installed across the country; some survive locally in one form or another. He died in 1811 at the age of 92.

M. Wane & Co., Edinbro', No. 87.

Preston Kirk.   near Dunbar.

18   Preston Mill is still a beautiful and much visited part of the county. Its tranquil nature made it very popular with both amateur and professional artists. Now, the National Trust for Scotland cares for the mill. It was working regularly at the turn of the century, the last survivor of many such mills on the Tyne. However, it suffered from frequent closure because it lies in the floodplain of the river. The wooden machinery, easily maintained, was powered by an undershot wheel, in turn driven by a lade from the nearby river. A key feature is a polygonal kiln with an 'oasthouse' ventilator capping the clay pantiles; the local weather meant it was necessary to dry the grain before milling. Just over the river is the farm of Phantassie, where John Rennie was born and his father was tenant farmer. John was the great engineer who (after a brief spell as a teacher in Dunbar) designed and built London Bridge and other engineering landmarks!

19   East Linton was and is very much an agricultural centre, which lay on both the Post Road and the main railway line. The parish of Prestonkirk held 17 arable farms at an average 380 acres of mostly top class land. The local tenant farmers' skill and enterprise were respected widely. Many worked more than a single steading; in his time the elder John Rennie was tenant of Markle, Markle Mains and Crauchie as well as Phantassie, a total of well over 1,500 acres. The photograph gives some idea that large fields are not just an invention of modern agro-businesses. Shelter belts of broad-leaved trees, like the foreground clump, were still essential. In olden days the building in the foreground was a perquisite of local landowners. It is a beehive doocot, or pigeon house. Their distribution was controlled strictly because the birds fed off the surrounding fields but the eggs, squabs and grown birds could bring welcome variety to the diet of the time.

East Linton.

20   East Linton presented a respectable face to the passer-by. It had barely a thousand inhabitants and so counted as little more than a village. But these fine frontages reflect its status as a 'Police Burgh'. Of old it was a burgh of baronry, with a baillie nominated by the Laird of Phantassie. Later, the administration was in the hands of a locally-elected council and magistrates with almost the same rights as an old 'Royal Burgh' such as Haddington or Dunbar. The only stir in the town was the annual near-riot when teams of Highland and Irish shearers assembled here for hire.

EAST LINTON

21　The rocky 'linn' in the foreground of this picture gives its name to the town. A low ridge of hard rock has created a bottleneck on the Tyne and a small but powerful cataract. The river can be forded closer to the sea but this place was ideal for a bridge to take the Post Road onwards to Edinburgh. The pent up waters were a valuable source of power for a number of grain and sawmills, some six of which were working at one time. Once, their output was channelled to a distillery, which also benefited from the plentiful water supply. At the time Victoria was crowned its output was 500,000 gallons annually, which was worth the sum of £120,000. Grain and malt poured into East Linton from all over the county; the product found its way to London via the harbours of Dunbar.

25737　　　**EAST LINTON FROM THE TYNE**　　　**VALENTINES SERIES**

22 The upstream side of the old bridge gives a good impression of the heart of the town. Views such as this attracted numerous artists to work here; it was mentioned that easels might match the rod from this point down to Preston Mill. Mention of the rod brings to mind another attraction of East Linton. In season, salmon made their way past the narrows and there were plenty of brown and sea trout in the river. Rights to take the fish were jealously guarded by land-owners along the riverside. One court case concerned an attempt to close a riverside right of way; it was believed that people on the path might just be using it to gain access to quiet corners for a bit of poaching (the pedestrians won). The substantial pier with its sharp cut-water has withstood floods where other bridges have failed – the first railway bridge, just a short way upstream, only lasted a year or two, being destroyed by floods in 1846. The new one and a road bypass have lasted longer.

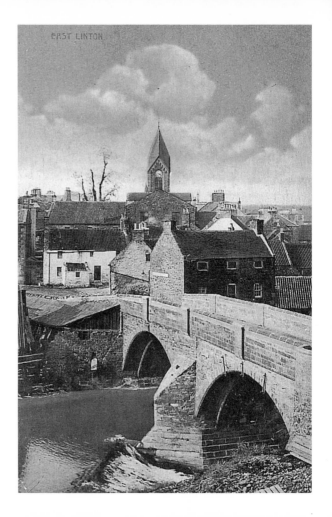

23   The fine sands of Belhaven Bay were once the port of Dunbar. Mediaeval trading craft were safely beached on the sand between tides and cargoes were handled directly to or from carts drawn up alongside. Larger boats were later to call directly at the walled harbours of Dunbar and by the early 19th century it took an expert surveyor to distinguish some faint signs of ancient usage. We know also that stone age people used the promontory on the right as a burial ground because cists have been eroded from its face. There was an attempt to promote a nearby spring as a spa, but this picture exemplifies the main use of the beach as viewing point and playground. The only boats to call here now would be toys floating in the Biel Burn. The bridge, built in 1886 and opened by Mrs. Anderson of Bourhouse, was properly called 'Seafield Bridge'. At high tide it is an island.

BELHAVEN SANDS, DUNBAR.

92005

24   Duke Street is a pleasant byway in Belhaven with, at the time of the picture, an interesting mixture of building styles. Some of these houses were available for summer let. Look carefully for a cross put on the card by the sender (who was enjoying the wonderful weather). It is just above the street lamp fixed close to the Skinyard wall on the right. This old name suggests that there might once have been a tanning industry in the village. That was long ago, but a Mrs. Norris operated her horse dealership near here for a few years during the First World War: more than a few of the animals would end up as hides and glue. The stairway in the left foreground shows how space could be best utilised in cramped conditions. This system made more available living space in the under-flat and so was a popular style. Watch out for more in other pictures.

Duke Street, Belhaven, DUNBAR

" Bisset Series."

25 Belhaven Brewery belonged to the Dudgeon family and has long been the largest business in the village. Its origins are lost in time but it is understood that a monastic settlement first used the local pure spring water hundreds of years ago. Lands in Belhaven were given to the monks of the May Island and the brewery buildings lie on land still called Monk's Croft. The Dudgeons were able to capitalise on motor transport to sell their award-winning ales farther afield. As a small family brewery it seems to have been too far away from Edinburgh (and perhaps it was too small) to be taken over by the big conglomerates of the post-war years. It has survived troubled times to expand its range of beers and their distribution.

26   After he retired William Kirkwood passed the time of day with his cronies about the street and his characteristic figure appears in several post-cards of Belhaven. He is on the extreme right here, on the corner of Brewery Lane, only a few steps away from his home at 12 High Street. The small general grocery behind is now a dwelling house, hav-ing gone the way of all the traditional stores and shops in Belhaven. And with the amount of vehicle traffic pass-ing up the hill to Dunbar, the corner is no longer the pleas-ant place it was. It still catches the morning sun, but the old boy's gang never meets for a pipe and a gossip.

27　This timeless picture shows the coast on a glorious evening. The way from Belhaven to the castle and harbour can be followed by paths within feet of the sea. Part of the route takes in the splendid promenade along the Heugh Heads beyond Winterfield. It is at its finest on long summer evenings when on the best of them the breeze dies away and the still air can be remarkably clear. In the distance North Berwick Law and the Bass Rock mark the entrance to the Firth of Forth. Sometimes remarkable optical effects can be seen – a common one is to experience the sight of the May Island upside down! Nearer at hand the rocky coast shelters a host of seabirds. Eider and mallard ducks can be seen on the Delves, a sea cut platform with many deep and treacherous channels where the sea is never still. Shags and divers frequent the Long Craigs, just off shore, perched with their drying wings outstretched. The only thing to disturb the peace are the hordes of gulls which follow returning fishing boats.

THE SETTING SUN FROM DUNBAR HARBOUR.　　　A 4885.

28   The doocot in the centre of Friars Croft is the most substantial remnant of a monastery of Red or Trinitarian Friars. It might originally have been a belfry and 18th century plans hint at the presence of more extensive ruins. The rest of the chapel, if it was, has been long since quarried away as building stone. It must have been built before the monastery was suppressed about 1529, which makes it well over 500 years old. From time to time, graves of those buried in the monastery's burial ground have come to light in the field. The white-washed cottages mark the limit of the Bleachfield created in 1756 on a part of the Inner Common. Bleaching fields were laid out in most East Lothian towns during that century and the facilities were useful even after the collapse of the linen industry. The farmyard was still well used when the photograph was taken, but in the present day it is simply a dwelling house.

29 The harbours of Dunbar are seen to their best advantage from the air, where they resemble a fish head, clasping Lamer Island in its mouth. Victoria Harbour was commenced in the 1840s to modernise port facilities. The 4½ acre basin was laid over two old landing places, Lamer and Castle Havens; they were little more than sandy areas between rocks, with perhaps wooden pole and plank wharves. On the west the new harbour is sheltered by the ancient castle and on the east by a Napoleonic battery on Lamer Island. The Battery was built by the authorities of the town against the depredations of seaborne marauders such as John Paul Jones and a noto- rious pirate, Captain Fall. Both had threatened the town. It became an isolation and fever hospital (used during periodic typhoid outbreaks at the Shore) until a tremendous storm ruined the buildings in the 1930s and has laid derelict ever since. The cost of the harbour almost bankrupted the town, until a levy on every burgh in Scotland and government grants paid off the debt.

Dunbar.

12901

30   This picture shows Tam Pat Johnston, James Tear, Bob Marr (and Jed) working with their lobster pots on the wharf of Victoria Harbour. The rocky coast of East Lothian is an ideal environment for edible crab and lobster. However, a fleet of pots needs constant attention. They are vulnerable to storms, which often spring up with little warning, and can end up strewn along the coast after particularly fierce ones. Once taken, the living harvest was stored in lidded, wooden fishboxes, such as the one in the foreground. The full ones could often be seen floating in the harbour in groups. By this means the catch would be kept fresh until a regular call from a fish merchant's dray and their dispatch to market (although, sometimes, one was hauled out to enable a local to make their choice). Bob became perhaps one of the most photographed people of the entire harbour community. He worked from a storeroom set into the chamber under the castle.

31   These fishers are from a generation before the last group. They may be waiting for the tide and their tranquillity belies the dangers of the task ahead. Look at their pipes with the bowl turned to the side for a good draw. There was a curious practice amongst the fishers (and some others), which was that then and now many people were known only by their by-names or nicknames. This helped to sort out who was who when there were only a few forenames in common use. There are several hundred known names, which have been collected and laid out in a poem or chant. Here are some (taken at random): Arry, Aipple, Boups, Callacher, Cud, Elicky, Gee Gee, Hillsixty, Paidler, Shie, Topsey, Traiveller, Tam Pat, Whitecraw and The Masher; amongst the women were found Tattie Soup and The Duchess. Goodness only knows how the names were all earned or derived, but many will be immediately familiar to those in the know.

32   The harshness of life as a fisherman cannot be emphasised enough, as Bob Paxton's face shows. Permanently burnt by sun, salt and cold, his gaze cuts across the years. The best of hard weather clothing available a century ago would be scorned by today's seafarers and fishers then would seldom afford the best. Heavy layers of wool and felt, tarpaulin over-trousers and tarred seaboots made any tumble into the sea a life-threatening scare. The vast majority of these men were non-swimmers. Losses at sea were regular occurrences: seven with the 'Tweed' in January 1895 (three were Paxtons); nine from the 'Golightly' in June 1886; coxswain Robert Herkes and Robert Clement from the lifeboat 'Wallace' on exercise in early 1877. Still, the losses were borne and sons followed fathers to the fishing and lifeboat service.

A SON OF THE SEA, DUNBAR. 47   SANSON'S SERIES, DUNBAR

33   The motorised lifeboat George and Sarah Strachan (1931) and her successors meant profound changes for the station and crews. The beachmen who had formerly assembled with the crews when the maroons went off were no longer needed. This force of up to 80 men had formerly been tasked with the launch of the boat. Their record, from resting to afloat, was 2 minutes 35 seconds. Their task had been tolerably easy when the boat was launched at the Broadhaven but other occasions had seen them well on the way to Hedderwick, or even further afield, before the horse teams were mustered. These days passed into the lore of the sta-tion. New technology placed increased demands on the crew in terms of skills and professionalism, a process which continues to the present day. The new boats had greater operating ranges, endurance and speed. Other stations nearby were closed, Skateraw amongst them, and Dunbar became responsible for greater sea areas. The nature of their rescues began to change as well, featuring more pleasure craft and fewer commercial vessels.

THE DUNBAR LIFEBOAT AND HARBOUR, DUNBAR.

34   This card exemplifies the (almost lost) pastime of strolling! Just look at the way the north pier of Victoria Harbour is thronged on a clear, warm summer's day. There may not be much to see in the harbour but it still seems to be worth taking a walk all the way along the pier's end, where the strollers might wonder at the ruins of the venerable castle and experience the sweep of the coast to the west. During the course of an afternoon they might be able to look down on departing fishing boats. The more adventurous types on top of the wall can see right to the Fife coast. Perhaps a few have cast a line for a fish or two. Down in the bottom right corner some youngsters have found something to interest them. Fragments of crabs, starfish and other sea life gathered in the cracks between the granite setts, leftovers from the catches which were dressed and prepared in the open air.

VICTORIA HARBOUR, DUNBAR.

35   Once safely back to port the hard work started. Nets were dried, overhauled and repaired, relaid and restowed. In older days each crewman got a share of the profit for each net he contributed to the boat. Subsequently, mechanical spinning and knotting by firms such as Stuart and Jacks of Musselburgh meant that nets were bought only by the owners. A top-end herring ring trawl, made from Egyptian cotton, could be 340 yards long and 70 score knots deep; with 72 knots to the yard, measured when the net was stretched, that means a depth of 20 yards. The top rope needed 500 corks and the bottom 240 lead sinkers. Tarred sisal was the fibre of choice for the cork and sole (bottom) ropes. To make it last the net could be treated by steeping in a solution of cutch ('barking' or tanning) and tarring, although this increased the weight by about 80 percent! The barking house at Dunbar was provided by the Town Council and leased to the fishers.

36 Tradition has it that the purse strings were firmly controlled by the womenfolk of the fishing community. Certainly believable in the case of 'True Blue', the rather determined looking lady here. Another tradition had a strictly practical purpose. Perhaps you can see a pattern knitted into the jersey worn by 'Brown' Johnston. These garments were knitted in the round and even the sleeves were knitted on so they were both tight-fitting and relatively waterproof. They had short-ish sleeves to keep the wrists out of the wet. Communities and families had their 'own' characteristic designs. Upper clothing lasted longest on corpses of lost fishers and a patterned jersey meant that found bodies could be repatriated, if not identified, and given decent burial in their own community. Dunbar's unique patterns appear to be lost and only parts of the designs are glimpsed in the detail of old photographs.

37 This photograph of the Old Harbour shows that it could handle fairly large craft. It was, however, quite a performance getting these boats to their berth through the narrow entrance. The harbour was probably laid out in the 16th century. Its basic line was improved by a grant from Cromwell's Parliament after he had found it inadequate and it has hardly changed since, despite periodic breaches in the seawall and alterations to the wharves. At one time the port had thirty trading craft, crewed by over 150 sailors, registered to it. These days passed long ago. The ship behind the men on the wharf was called 'Firebrick' and recalls the trade in drainage pipes from the Seafield Brickworks at West Barns to Holland. The return cargo was red pantiles, which still roof many of the farm steadings around the town. It may just be possible, with a careful look, to make out the lighthouse at he end of the pier. It was removed many years ago.

38   William Brodie of Battleblent raised £112 in 1856 to provide an essential public barometer for the fishing community. Fifty years on it was still in pristine condition, looked after by a succession of volunteers who appreciated both the beauty of Handysides Ritchie's carving and the utility of the barometer. The decoration showed the fruits of the sea and a figurative wharfside scene. The barometer can be seen in the previous picture situated in front of the harbourmaster's pokey little office at the corner of Cromwell Harbour. It became a popular stop on the tourist round. There was always a hoary old son of the sea willing to pose for a photograph (for a consideration) or able to spin a tale (for a fill of 'baccy'). A grand way to pass the time and a sunny day, watching the coming and going in the busy harbour. It's quiet now, the office is long gone and the plinth is dilapidated and eroding in the wind.

M. Wane & Co., Edinbro', No. 84.

Weather Glass,   Dunbar.

39   Hugh White established his joinery and cartwright firm in 1885. In 1913 the company occupied a yard between Lamer and Colvin (once Coffin) Streets. This little family firm was able to make all kinds of vehicles. In the example here, the body has been fitted to the bare chassis. Traditional wheelwrights and coach builders worked alongside mechanics, engineers and metal workers. The skills of journeymen were passed to apprentices, who learnt their trades and became the garage owners and their staff in the next generation. Skilled men were also in demand for the manufacture of agricultural equipment. From 1804 at the Dunbar foundry, John and George Sked supplied steam engines and threshing mills. By the start of this century Thomas Sherriff of West Barns and David Wilson of East Linton built an amazing range of state of the art implements for ploughing and sowing or reaping and packing.

40   The sands at the East Beach are conveniently placed. The photograph shows that the bay is cradled by the ridge on which the town sits; it is scarcely 100 yards from the High Street. It can be seen also that a number of the bigger hotels were near at hand. The Roxburghe and Bellevue are the largest buildings on the horizon. The fine, golden sand is perfect for sandcastles and competitions were held regularly every summer right up to the 1960s. A shallow, shelving spit ran between two rocky arms and provided a safe space for paddling – at least when the sea was calm. The groyne built on one of the rock ridges helps to retain the sand. These same rocks might be the ones where John Muir found 'invisible, boy-devouring monsters' lurking in the rockpools during the games he and his friends played by the seaside. Before the seawall on the right was built the road to Woodbush, the huddle of small buildings, ran along the sand.

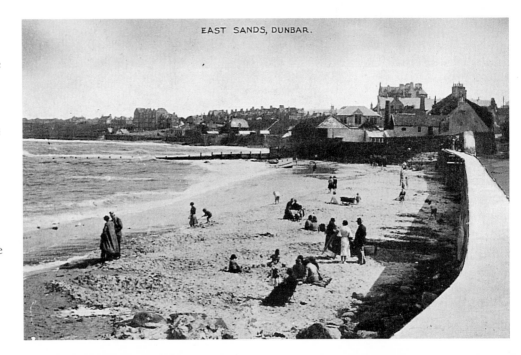

EAST SANDS, DUNBAR.

41   The Cats' Row was a curious line of tenements running from Victoria Street to the Broadhaven. This single block housed a considerable proportion of the entire fishing community. This suited the close-knit families very well for many years but the owners seemed to be content to let the properties deteriorate and they were eventually condemned and cleared away. Old photographs show that a large part of the lives of the residents was spent outside in the street, whether it be household tasks or working at baiting the lines and repairing fishing tackle. Consequently, there are many photographs of the area. A single old building, the Rock House, stood isolated by itself, on the left above. The story was that this was where John Wesley, the founding father of Methodism, resided when in Dunbar. The chapel stands close to here and is one of the oldest such worship places in Scotland; it was built in 1764, which means Rock House must have been much older.

The Cats' Row, Dunbar,   Valentine's Series

42   Rather than follow the Dawell Brae or Silver Street back uphill to the High Street an inquisitive visitor could take one of the 'closes'. There are many of them. The ones on the west side of the High Street lead only to private gardens but most of those on the east side were common thoroughfares. As such, they were completely different in character from the wider streets they linked, evocative of a much earlier time. This photograph clearly shows their structure – a narrow lane beside a wall dividing the tenement lands, flanked with a row of tiny cot-houses or workshops and usually passing under the building that fronted the main street.

Their names recalled function – Old Post Office, Old Bank or Slaughterhouse Closes – or a proprietor – Baillie Simpson's, Bookless', Logan's or Forrest's Closes. This is Johnstone's Close and it was also known as the Irish Close, in consequence of the lodging houses (on the right) used by itinerant labourers.

1933.   JOHNSTONE'S CLOSE, DUNBAR.

43 Many of the visitors in the late 19th century would make a point of attending the kirk during their stay and often visiting divines would be called on to preach a sermon. This fine view of the Established Kirk was originally published in a book of photographs showing popular local views. By the time postcards came along ten years later the picture was out of date. Local readers will be aware that the eastern end of the kirk was changed by the addition of a protruding, five-sided apse, or chancel. The building itself replaced an earlier kirk and was consecrated in 1821. The first kirk had stood since 1342, if not before (there was certainly a church in Dunbar in 1176), and had grown draughty and dilapidated. It was cleared away and the new one stands on exactly the same site. Many of the gravestones in this picture are still standing. However, the constant wind has eroded all detail from some and carved fantastic shapes into others.

44   Barns Ness Lighthouse warns the unwary of the shelving coast at Cat Craig. Once, the keepers stationed here were the front line defenders of coastal traffic. Nowadays it is untended, the light is less powerful and more reliance is placed on technology. However, the coast is still as dangerous and to sailing craft in a north-easterly wind this is a perilous lee shore. It has seen countless wrecks. Two Royal Navy frigates, Pallas and La Nymphe, were wrecked here on the same winter night in December 1810, mistaking the fires of Cat Craig and Oxwellmains lime kilns for the May light, in reality much farther away. (This was almost as much a loss as the French inflicted in that entire year.) A generation later the wreck of Le Rodeur of Belgium, bound for Glasgow with a cargo of apples, was remembered even more years later by John Muir. He does not say if he remembers the many deaths along the coast that same night on five or six more wrecks.

45   The Lifeboat Station was augmented in 1907 by the stationing of a second boat at Skateraw using a crew from Dunbar. A bazaar raised the £300 necessary to purchase a 35 ft Liverpool class boat, the 'Sarah Kay'. The coxswain for both stations was the serving Dunbar coxswain Walter Fairbairn (standing here), and the training of two second coxswains ensured that both boats were operational at all times. Fairbairn, who came of a fisher family from Cove, retired in 1931 having been 37 years elected coxswain and fifty years on the lifeboats. He won a Silver Medal for gallantry in 1905 and was instrumental in saving over 180 lives in his career. The 'Sarah Kay' was retained in service until 1943 by which time she was the last sailing and pulling boat in Scotland with 16 service launches and 57 lives to her credit. The boathouse was closed when she went.

SKATERAW LIFEBOAT, DUNBAR.

46   Even today Cove Harbour is a well-kept secret. A small harbour is tucked in a tiny bay under high cliffs. A few close-knit families made their living from the sea. The slope on the inland side of the harbour wall made a convenient place to careen and repair boats. This picture shows a tunnel running into the cliff; it gave onto ample storage spaces for nets and equipment. The fishermen of this coast had once a reputation as great smugglers (hand in glove with the local merchants, of course). Cove fishers were notorious for their skill in landing, hiding and disposing of brandy, tobacco and other commodities. The customs station was at Dunbar and on a dark night, with the excise men far away, nowhere could be better than Cove for landing illicit cargoes from darkened merchantmen standing off the coast. These caves were used to enhance the tales, but are the more prosaic result of old attempts to work thin coals underlying this end of the county.

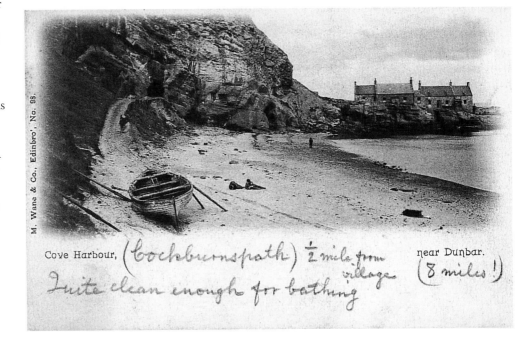

M. Wane & Co., Edinbro', No. 98.

Cove Harbour, (Cockburnspath) ½ mile from village   near Dunbar. (8 miles!)
Quite clean enough for bathing

47 The dog has seen it all before but is still interested, perhaps wondering what might go wrong this time. Cove was already in decline as a working harbour. It had suffered disproportionate losses of boats and men in a few short years. Many were amongst the 189 men lost in the Great East Coast Disaster of October 1881 (in 1917 there were still fifty widows and dependants receiving annuities). Most of the survivors gave up their larger boats and fished close to home. However, as picture 45 shows, one Cove man, Walter Fairbairn, rose above the adversities that had struck his community. The group of fishermen here have turned out to launch one of their beached cobles. The method is the same the world over. Some steady the boat and others arrange a set of wooden rollers down the slope. The cable is hauled and the boat slides ponderously towards the water's edge, with youngsters scampering to bring rollers from behind to the front as soon as they are free.

48   This view places the harbour in relation to the surrounding cliffs. It also gives a closer view of the cottages at the harbour, and makes clear their precarious siting. The Berwickshire cliffs lead down to Fast Castle, another place with a murky reputation and tales of smuggling and buried treasure. This stretch of coastline was much frequented by amateur geologists. They came to follow in the footsteps of the greats whose investigations along the coastal strata laid the basis of the modern science. A route from Siccar Point past Greenheugh and Red Rock to Cove is still walked by first-year students from Edinburgh University. The harbour entrance can be made out. It took three attempts to build the breakwater, storms taking the first two. But the man behind the project, Sir James Hall of Dunglass, was a determined chap and he tried again, taking his theme from Bruce and the spider.

No. 101.

THE SHORE, COCKBURNSPATH

49   Pease Glen widens just enough to fit in a mill steading beside the sea. The in-bye grazing land, well drained and sheltered, was a perfect location for summer camps and it was seldom without its quota campers and picnickers. At first there were volunteers and militia on summer maneuvers. On other occasions the fields held Sunday schools, factory work forces and their families and sometimes the populations of whole towns. Scout troops were formed across the county by 1910 and they found such sites ideal for their activities. If you look closely beside the octagonal, pantiled mill roof, you might make out that there is a race in progress across the field. Countryside camps and events were organised down to the minute with a vast range of competitions. There were so many that surely everybody would have some chance at one of the many prizes on offer.

No. 100.

PEASE GLEN AND MILL, COCKBURNSPATH.

50   A figure caught in the moonlight gazes into the depths of the beautifully wooded Pease Glen, a classic Edwardian picture which exploits the romantic reputation of the valley. Although just within Berwickshire, it was often regarded as part of East Lothian. Together with Dunglass Dean it formed a barrier to north-south traffic, which meant that in times past the south-eastern flank of the Dunbar area was readily defended. There was an old coastal road, little more than a track, which was not surpassed until this bridge was built in 1786. The main span is 300 ft and there is a drop at the central pier of 120 ft to the valley below. Until the railways stretched across the land it was one of the highest bridges in the country.

Pease Bridge near Dunbar.

51 Cockburnspath, or sometimes Coldbrandspath, is too much of a mouthful. Everyone uses Co'path. East of Dunbar, it is a pretty little village that, although in Berwickshire, naturally looked to Dunbar as the nearest market town. Its people were mainly agricultural workers, rural artisans and the small traders that kept them in household goods and such foodstuffs that were not available from the land. Co'path was once entitled to hold official markets in its own right, but the practice was not economic by the time this photo was taken. The market cross is a fine example of the symbols that once stood in every market place. Few survive in their original state; others are romantic Victorian (or later) revivals. This one makes a pleasant place to sit and show off the grandchildren. Look at the wear in the stones at the bottom tier.

THE OLD MARKET CROSS, COCKBURNSPATH

52   The Hotel at Co'path was at a convenient distance from Dunbar to make a nice rest stop. Its main function had been a coaching inn, supplying fresh teams to the mail coaches hurrying along the Post Road between Edinburgh and the border. It lost this trade to the railway. The construction of the line lent Co'path something of the aspect of a 'frontier town' from the old 'wild' west. The navvies on the Linton-Dunglass section were camping locally and 'amused' themselves in the village. Special constables and the military had to be mustered to control the shenanigans. As the tourist industry grew the hotel adapted very well to the new trade.

For many years the landlord was William Nisbet (later of the Old Ship Inn in Dunbar). He ensured a convivial welcome for all who stopped by and earned a reputation far beyond the immediate neighbourhood – the sender of this card had cycled all the way from North Berwick; it would be a good thirty miles round trip.

The Hotel, Cockburnspath.

53   A photographer with an eye towards the romantic composed this picture, capturing an old corner of Co'path. The architecture shows a mixture of styles, from the typical outside stair to the single-story cottages. The white-washed wall probably marks out the corner as the site of a midden, cleaned away only on the visit of a scavenger's cart. The path is roughly cobbled and would lead to a rutted farm track with no made-up surface. Only the principal thoroughfares were made up to a high standard, which meant that skilled drivers were worth the hire on an excursion. Hill parish roads also suffered from high farm traffic –

droves of animals, all kind of carts, agricultural equipment of every description. The artist who coloured the card was not aware that most roofs were tiled with red clay pantiles and coloured them all slate-grey. In black and white it does not matter anyway!

54 Dunglass Chapel was a great attraction for day trippers. It dated to the 15th century when it was built for the Humes, whose tower was nearby. Over the years they added to its beauty and endowments. One of them erected it into a collegiate church to ensure prayers for his family would be said in perpetuity. However, Sir James Hall, a later proprietor, stripped it out to use as a stable. Most of the bodies buried inside were dug up and the bones thrown away. Many of the gravestones were broken up for other use. One of the results was the gaping entrance created in the east end, for the use of his carts. He even used the aisle where his wife and only son were buried to store fodder for animals stabled in the nave. The whole affair caused a great stir, not least on the part of the late owners. Later owners were more sympathetic and the ruin still provided many features to interest visiting antiquarians.

Dunglass Chapel, Cockburnspath.

55 In John Muir's account of his boyhood and youth we get a graphic picture of the fun that could be had by the youngsters of Dunbar. Summer days were for escaping from the town to the rural byways, racing at full pelt along the country roads to the steadings and hillside glens. There were nests to hunt in the woodlands and bushes. The plentiful hill streams provided lots of interesting tadpoles, frogs, or minnows and under the banks there were bigger fish to try to guddle. With a 'jeely-jar' one might take home all manner of crawling beasties. Of course, they would never be allowed indoors with their treasures, but they could always try.

There was always lots to see in farmyards. If a farmer slaughtered a pig, there would always be a pack of boys on hand. They were attracted by the squeals and would be hoping for the unfortunate animal's bladder. Inflated, it made a fine football.

The Ford Oldhamstocks. Photo by Bruce Redding

56 The village of Oldhamstocks stands like a ribbon along its narrow road, terraced on the steep north bank of a burn and out of sight until the very last moment. Now very quiet indeed, it was and is the nucleus of an agricultural parish. Here were found the church and school, a few shops, a blacksmith or two and a farrier, and an inn. The neat little houses reflect the fertility of the agricultural land in East Lothian and the progressive inclinations of farmers and landowners. No sign here of the sod houses with heather thatch that were still to be found in other rural parts of Scotland. Oldhamstocks parish dealt mainly in livestock and fodder crops. A bit of game and forestry provided variety amongst the inland pasturelands. Down by the sea the arable lands cropped potatoes, carrots and turnips (some of the highest quality produce in Scotland). Underlying the land are reserves of ironstone, limestone, some coal and good quality building stone.

Old Hamstocks, Cockburnspath.

57   It is probably plain that there are lots of local names dating from the time the district was part of a Dark Ages Northumbrian kingdom. Innerwick is one such, so there has been a settlement here for a very long time, exploiting the fertile coastal plain and grazing land in the higher hill pastures; certainly, ancient burials have been found from time to time. Just as Oldhamstocks, the village is tucked away from the coast so that it is out of sight from any great distance. In times past seclusion was the best defense for these little villages. There had been a small castle nearby which belonged to a branch of the Hamiltons and a little farther away was the old castle of Thurston. Nearby to the latter a minister of Innerwick had an encounter with the ghost of the Laird of Cool. The story was published and told again and again in the district. No doubt it was embellished each time.

The Village, Innerwick

58   This is where the second great battle of Dunbar was fought on the morning of 3 July 1650 between the troops of the Scots General Leslie and those of Oliver Cromwell. Leslie had roundly out-manoeuvred Cromwell for weeks, forcing the latter to fall back on Dunbar for supplies and rest. Most of his troops were ill and he feared a stand-to fight. Leslie kept him pinned by holding the high ground of Doon Hill and blockading the south with cavalry. But the regimented stooks of newly-reaped grain echo the ranks of the Scots after they left the high ground and deployed on the open land below. This unfortunate move delivered them into the hands of Cromwell's battle-hardened men. After an in-conclusive start, they were able to penetrate weaknesses in the Scots line and roll up the front, chivvying and harrying the resulting rabble all the way up the side of the valley. It only took two hours to kill 3,000 and capture a further 10,000 Scots.

DUNBAR. — Oswaldean and Doon Hill the position occupied by the Scottish Army. Battle of Dunbar 1650

59 The Beach Improvement Committee was formed in 1878. It brought together a diverse group of interests in the civic, commercial and sporting fields. Its work was very effective and two groynes were soon in place to retain a greater depth of sand on the East Beach. Two bridges were sited to cross the Biel Burn at Belhaven and West Barns. No less than five bathing places were designated and improved – hardly the swimming ponds of later days, but an advance on bathing from the beaches where swimmers were at the mercy of the tides and offshore currents. At first the sexes were strictly segregated and the Old Bathe, first mentioned in the 1840s, became the Gentlemen's Bathing Pool. There was already a retaining wall so it was fitted with a one-way valve to improve the change-over of water. Out on the rocks a pathway was carved and a handrail and ladder were installed for adult seabathers. Inshore, a gentle sandy bottom was ideal for young beginners!

DUNBAR. THE OLD BATHE.   78537

60   Opening Day! Dunbar Town Council embarked on a great programme of public works in the 1920s. The town now had a 'Civic Improvement Committee' to coordinate action. Inadequate housing in the old part of the burgh was replaced by new 'schemes' (housing estates) in the Boroughdales. Tennis courts and putting greens, capable of hosting competitions of forty couples or 500 putters respectively, appeared in all suitable places; the income of over £500 annually helped to defray their cost. The jewel in the crown was undoubtedly the 'Safety Swimming Pond', seen here at its debut gala on 29th June 1929. 500,000 gallons of refreshing (icy, even in high summer) sea water was filtered and frequently changed in a secure, well-finished basin. There were terraces for spectators, latecomers making do with the slopes of the Glebe, and in 1930 the old pavilion made way for a suitably modern affair, with all mod cons.

THE SAFETY SWIMMING POND DUNBAR (THE LARGEST IN SCOTLAND)   206461.J.V.

61 This is what a trip to the seaside at Dunbar meant for sixty years. This fact is attested to by many recent visitors who, returning after many years, look in vain for their old playground. The whole bay has been returned to nature, but at its peak in the pre-war years the pool complex boasted paddling and boating ponds, the main pool and this stunning pavilion. It was built of red stone and it held changing rooms, offices, a snack bar (selling essential hot drinks) and a large function room. The ballroom and terrace hosted dances in the long summer evenings. Every week during the summer there were all manner of competitions and galas. A team of 'grotesque' divers made regular appearances and renowned British swimmers gave exhibitions of their skill. The photograph shows that the pool was busy even on ordinary days. Several sets of chutes and diving boards provided variety – some were at the deep end and some at the shallow side for the youngsters.

214785. J.V. DUNBAR BATHING POND AND NEW PAVILION.

62 Unfortunately, the best-laid plans of the Council and Corporation of Dunbar were let down by the drama of the sea at their chosen site. The unpredictability of summer storms meant that a good swim was never a sure thing. The seawall under the line of breakers was systematically raised, but to no avail. Consequently, the pool was often a good three or four feet deeper than designed. Weed, sand and stones were brought to the pool bottom by every wave, leading to frequent, laborious cleaning operations. However, in circumstances such as here, youngsters could still have a fine time. Rather than perch on the diving platforms, the very best place to view the waves was the hulk of the Doo Rock, upper right. Of course, getting there was half the fun. The lee of the seawall made a perfect suntrap when the waves subsided and was a very popular place to spread a towel and bask on summer afternoons.

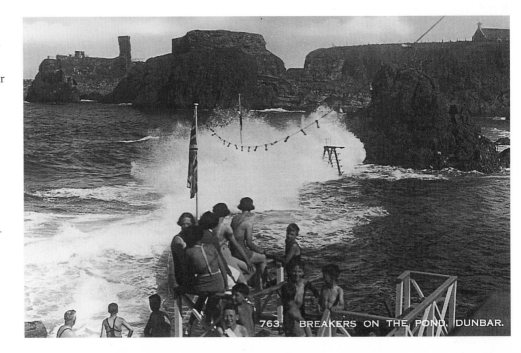

763. BREAKERS ON THE POND, DUNBAR.

63 The New Bowling Green was pretty old, even when this photo was taken. The 'new' was named in relation to an 'old', which was laid out where the Abbey Church was built. These lands were once part of a Maison Dieu or hostel associated with the Collegiate Church of Dunbar; the new green was on part of the Minister's Glebe with the kirkyard directly behind the ivy-covered wall. The club was well situated to catch the holiday trade because the entrance is in Station Road. A monthly membership of 5 shillings was offered to summer visitors. The Municipal Course in Lauderdale Park offered membership at the rate of a half-crown per month (half the amount). In the background is the appropriately named Bellevue Hotel, one of Dunbar's largest. It was a landmark building standing high on the Kirkhill and virtually all the rooms had a commanding view over the surrounding countryside and seascape.

Dunbar, New Bowling Green

G. Grahame, Dunbar.

64   Winterfield Park was opened on land given to the town. In those days it was the New Park. There were two older parks but Castle Park was occupied by the military for most of the summer and Cowan's Park, beside the Bleachfield, was unsuitable for more than a few sports (the cricket club played there). Here, however, were new tennis courts, putting greens and wide fields. It was inaugurated by a great summer gala in 1925, but more to the point it provided space for organised groups of excursionists from the cities. They would assemble from their train and march through the town, often with a band. The pavilion in the park pro- vided all mod cons and there was space for marquees and all manner of sporting activities. For many years groups of entertainers leased the pavilion for variety shows. To some extent, this kept them and their (noisy) audiences away from the town centre.

TENNIS COURTS AND PAVILIONS, PUBLIC PARK, DUNBAR.   38638.J.V.

65 After sightseeing, the day might be reprised on a stroll through Lochend Woods. The woodlands were preferred by many for their peaceful quietness far away from the bustle of the Public Park and the town. The estate lies just beyond the burgh boundaries and belonged to the Warrender family. They were also the proprietors of the Marchmont district of Edinburgh. Deep within the woods was the remnant of their ancient house, but no more than a wing remained after a fire took hold during a gale. A fine gateway, perhaps part of a chapel, was all that indicated the past grandeur of the house. The Lover's Walk is one of a network of paths running through the estate connecting Eweford to Goldenstones and the Latch Park to the Plunderland Butts. One of the nearby fields was called St. John's Croft recalling, as does Templelands on the High Street, an ancient connection with the Knights Templar.

Lovers Walk, Lochend, Dunbar.

66   In the Middle Ages the lordship of Spott was in the gift of the Earls of Dunbar and March and was held usually by their Steward or Castellan. At the core of the present house is an ancient tower built on massive foundations. It was one of the strongpoints that supported the central fortress of Dunbar. Similar towers stud the landscape of East Lothian but most are bare ruins. Others like Spott Tower were changed and adapted. In the early nineteenth century a full scale renovation by Mr. Sprott of Spott, as he was styled, gave the house its outward Scots Baronial look. The pretty decoration and gentle gardens deceive the eye, because the building is on a spur protruding into a ravine. It is now bridged on two sides but once it was enhanced by a moat, a position of great strength.

Spott House

67   It might not be believed from this tranquil scene of a ploughman and his pair of horses heading for home down the main street of Stenton, but the village has secrets. While some visitors might be drawn by antiquarian pursuits others came in search of the macabre. For the first group there are standing stones and ancient camps in the hills showing the great antiquity of settlement, battlefields to be walked and history to be sought out. But these hill parishes had black reputations for witch burning, a practice which continued here for longer than other parts of the lowlands. One Bessie Knox and four others were convicted and died here at the stake in 1659. There were similar events in all the places nearby, especially Spott.

Stenton, East.

68   Pressmennan Lake was made in 1819 by damming a little stream in a long narrow valley in the hills behind Stenton. Never more than a couple of hundred yards wide, it is over a mile long. As this photograph shows, one never sees its full extent. The shoreline hugs the tree-clad contour, creating bays and headlands along its sinuous length. 'By the kind permission of the landowner' (as it says with due deference in the old guidebooks) Victorian and Edwardian holiday makers were able to walk in the woods and picnic and play in the meadows. Here they could get away from the ever-present breeze by the coast and experience the full strength of the summer sun. A little way along the valley a hillside spring gave abundant refreshingly pure water – it is still in use today; the same guidebook mentions it is best mixed with a few drops of 'tincture', whatever that might mean! The lake held some of the best trout in East Lothian, stocked from Loch Leven by the owner.

69   This photograph and the next provide an interesting contrast. The old lands of Whittingham, the largest parish in East Lothian, were held by the Earls of Dunbar and March. It was their successors who built the tower in the late 15th century. The new owners were a branch of the Douglas family, later the Earls of Morton. Visitors with antiquarian interests came to speculate about the plot to assassinate Darnley, which was hatched here between Bothwell, Lethington and Morton. An ancient yew was held to have been the exact place where the deed was planned. The tree was still being pointed out in 1891 when its branches had the remarkable circumference of 312 ft.

Old Tower Whittingehame (5½ miles from Dunbar)

70 Whittingehame was purchased by James Balfour in 1817. The new house was built on the family's Indian fortune and remained their seat for a number of years during which time a vast estate was assembled. A later occupant was of course Arthur Balfour, the Prime Minister. His yacht is prominent in many old pictures of Victoria Harbour at Dunbar. Two of the most important hands on the estate were William Rintoul and his successor, a Mr. Garrett, the gardeners under whose management the grounds were laid out and improved until they were 'a treat to visit and admire', as an old account stated. The parish bears another of the local 'Northumbrian' place-names. You may note that it is spelt differently in this account; the version with two letter 'e's was popularised when the Balfours had the estate.

M. Wane & Co., Edinbro', No. 204.

Whittingham.

Nr. Dunbar.

71   Not all the rural housing matched that which visitors would see in villages like Oldhamstocks or Tyninghame. Bella, Mary, Grace and Agnes are at the door of their home at Burnfoot near Stenton. The cottage was let to their father during the time that he worked on the Biel Estate. Such cottages might once have been thatched, with one end used as a byre, and for a while it was also traditional to take fittings such as windows along with all the rest of the furniture from let to let. The incoming tenants would find only the bare shell. This house was not a popular place to stay as records show a rapid turnover of occupants. The children probably went to school at Stenton village while they were at this house, but the next term could find them starting again at a new school, if their father took new employment. The picture may have been taken by William Nisbet of nearby Lint Mill, who made a reputation as a photographer after building his first camera in the 1860s.

72   Biel House is shown here at the height of its splendour. Viewed from the south the terraced garden runs down to Biel Water and an extensive, well-stocked Deer Park. Once again, a Georgian frontage hides an ancient tower, which was extended at different times both west and east. The land once belonged to the Dunbars, then it went to Robert Lauder of the Bass and his family, then to a branch of the Hamiltons, of whom one was the staunch antagonist to the Union, Lord Belhaven. One of the treasures once kept in the house was a prayer book used by the Archbishop of Canterbury at the marriage of George III and many subsequent royal baptisms and marriages. Perhaps of greater note was a large collection of old masters, including Vandykes and Gainsboroughs. The house was altered considerably in 1952.

M. Wane & Co., Edinbro', No. 92.

Beil House,   Dunbar.

73 The approaches to Biel were ideal to Victorian eyes, like this pleasant avenue through mature trees. Through these woodland ways could be glimpsed the rich fields of the surrounding farms: amongst them How-muir, Hedderwick, Ninewar, Biel Grange and Pitcox. Between the latter and Bower-house, just by the Pleasants Farm road was a cottage with the wonderful old name Hurkletillane, meaning 'the well on the hill'. Some of these nearby woods hide un-expected delicacies. The story starts in Italy. This was where a stock of beech seedlings was purchased to reforest the estates. Along with the soil there came associated fungi. Those in the know do not tell where, but exotic truffles can still be found and readily find a market in the restaurants of Edinburgh.

M. Wane & Co., Edinbro', No. 85.

Avenue at Biel.   Dunbar.

74   This was a common experience on a country jaunt – a watersplash. Many of the little country roads crossed the small rivers tumbling down from the Lammermuirs by simply plunging straight across; some still do! The estates around Dunbar enjoyed a considerable degree of seclusion despite the tourist carriages thronging the rural byways in the summer months. All main routes into and out of esates were guarded by lodges at the places roads intercepted boundary walls or as here, the fords. The walls often ran around the perimeter of the Mains (or home) farm as well as the immediate grounds of the big houses and their various wildernesses, deer parks, and grass parks. The lodges were leased to the outdoor estate servants – especially the gamekeeper and his staff. One of the reasons for this security was the popularity of game shooting amongst the land owning classes. Their right to shoot over the land was rigorously enforced by licensing all guns and bringing all those caught poaching up before the County Magistrates.

Biel Bill-Ford (5 Miles from Dunbar)

G. Grahame, Dunbar

75   There are essential sea-walls from East Links to the mouth of Victoria Harbour, above, where ferocious waves lash the north side of the wall. Shipping was once protected from damage by barricading the entrances with timber booms. However, waves in a good tearing gale can rise high above the harbour wall, rather negating the effect. The best solution was to move all craft to the Old Harbour and wait it out. Many boats have come to grief on these rocks, often in sight of spectators on the castle rock, having failed to make the entrance. Although it was impossible to launch the lifeboat in conditions like this (a lesson hard learnt) the Rocket Brigade came into their own. A line and breeches buoy were then rigged, if all went well, to bring the stranded to shore. In a sea like this second coxswain Herkes of the lifeboat swam to untangle such a line, a feat that saved the lives of twenty people.

AN EASTERLY GALE, DUNBAR.   219698

76   It might be best to end at the Shore with a reminder of past riches won from the sea. The port was the station of choice for the east coast herring fleet many years; in those times it was said that one could walk from one side of the harbour to the other on the ranks of fishing craft. All that is past and now there are few boats sailing from the harbours. In 1920, when this card was posted, the departure of the boats to the fishing grounds were still a daily routine watched from Lamer Island by curious sightseers and perhaps anxious relatives. The latter knew well the caprice of the stormy North Sea. Bear in mind the previous picture and place this little yawl in the scene. The words once written above the Fisherman's's Barometer (picture 38) take on deeper significance: 'presented to the fishermen of Dunbar to whose perilous industry the burgh owes so much of its prosperity'.

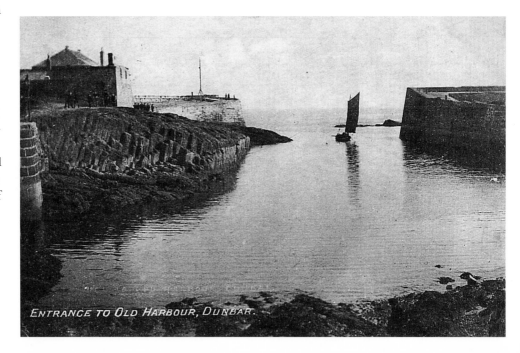

ENTRANCE TO OLD HARBOUR, DUNBAR.